This Book Belongs To

_____

THE FIRST CHRISTMAS

By Solveig Muus and Bart Tesoriero

Illustrated by Michael Adams

ISBN 978-1-61796-304-9
Library of the Congress Control Number 2018966927
Artwork © 2019 Michael Adams, Text © 2019 Aquinas Kids
Printed in China

Once upon a time, many years ago, there was a lovely young woman named Mary. She lived with her mother and father in a small town called Nazareth, in the land of Israel.

In those days, people felt very lonesome for God. They said to one another, "I wonder if God really loves us?" They wished that God did not seem so far away. The people felt sad, too, because no matter what they did, they knew they could never be good enough for a holy God.

However, all hope was not lost, because God had a plan. Through the years, God sent holy men, called prophets, to tell His people about a savior He would send. He would be the Messiah, the man God anointed to set His people free. One of the greatest prophets, Isaiah, proclaimed that the Messiah would be born of a virgin, and he would be called Immanuel, which means "God with us." Another prophet, Micah, announced that the Messiah would be born in Bethlehem.

God had a very special plan for Mary. And now it was time for His plan to begin. It was time for the Messiah to come.

*T*hus it came to pass that one day an angel named Gabriel appeared to Mary and said, "Hail Mary! You are full of grace. Do not be afraid, for the Lord is with you!" Mary was troubled when she heard these words. She wondered what sort of greeting it was.

Gabriel told Mary that she had found favor with God. She was a princess in His eyes. Gabriel said, "Behold, you will conceive in your womb and bear a son, and you shall name him Jesus."

Mary gasped. God wanted her to bear His Son! Mary said to the angel, "How can this be, since I am a virgin? I have never had relations with a man." The angel answered, "The Holy Spirit will come upon you, and the power of the Most High will overshadow you. Therefore the child to be born will be called holy, the Son of God. Behold, Elizabeth, your relative, is also going to have a child in her old age. Nothing is impossible for God." Mary replied, "Behold, I am the servant of the Lord. May it be done unto me as you have said." Then the angel left her.

Mary had a hard time sleeping that night, thinking about all that had happened that day. She felt nervous, yet so thrilled! This was not an easy decision, but Mary trusted God. He would give her the strength she needed.

When Mary awoke the next morning, she was filled with joy. For a moment, it seemed like the angel's visit had been a dream. It seemed quite impossible, but Mary was a woman of deep faith, and she knew it was true.

Mary remembered that the angel said that her cousin, Elizabeth, was expecting a child. Elizabeth and her husband Zechariah had wanted so badly to have a baby, but were never able to do so. How wonderful that God had granted their wish and answered their prayers! Yet Elizabeth was elderly and would need help. Right away, Mary decided to visit her. She quickly got ready and set off on the long journey to the hill country of Judea where her cousin lived.

It took Mary a few days to travel the distance, so when she arrived at the home of Zechariah and Elizabeth, she was very weary from the long journey. Mary got off the donkey and entered the house. She called out, "Elizabeth!"

When Elizabeth heard Mary's voice, the baby inside her jumped with joy! At that moment, Elizabeth was filled with the Holy Spirit. She cried out, "Most blessed are you among women, and blessed is the baby you carry! Who am I, that the mother of my Lord should come to me? Blessed are you for believing that what the Lord spoke to you would come to pass!"

Mary was betrothed, or engaged, to Joseph, a carpenter in Nazareth. In those days, two people were considered to be married as soon as they promised themselves to each other. However, the custom was to wait for one year after they were betrothed until they lived together.

Joseph's ancestor was King David, but he lived many years earlier, and any family wealth was long gone. Now Joseph had to work as hard as he could to make a living. Still, he and Mary were looking forward to a quiet life together in Nazareth.

When Mary returned home after spending three months with her cousin Elizabeth, it was obvious she was pregnant. Joseph, her husband, was a good man, but troubled by her condition. Although Joseph was not the father of the child, he did not want to put Mary to shame. Therefore he decided to send her away quietly.

That night, Joseph fell into a deep sleep. The angel of the Lord came to Joseph in a dream. The angel said, "I have come to tell you that Mary, your betrothed, will have a son sent by God. You are to name him Jesus, because he will save his people from their sins." When he heard this, Joseph was surprised, and also a little afraid, but he was faithful to the Lord. When he awoke, Joseph followed the angel's direction. He took Mary into his home and cared for her tenderly.

Mary was very thankful that Joseph had taken her into his home. She worked hard to keep it clean and nice, and to prepare it for the baby when the time came. Joseph built a sturdy crib, and Mary knit blankets that would keep the baby warm during the cold Nazareth nights.

Mary felt great consolation when she remembered that it was the Holy Spirit who revealed to Elizabeth that the child in Mary's womb was holy, the Son of God Himself. Mary had responded to Elizabeth with a great song of praise, saying,

"My soul proclaims the greatness of the Lord, and my spirit rejoices in God my Savior. For He has looked with favor upon the lowliness of his servant."

"Surely," Mary said, "from now on people of all generations will call me blessed. The Mighty One has done great things for me, and holy is His name. His mercy is from age to age to those who fear Him. He has shown strength with His arm, and He has scattered the proud in the thoughts of their hearts. He has brought down the rulers from their thrones and has lifted up the lowly. He has filled the hungry with good things, and the rich He has sent empty away. He has helped His servant Israel, remembering His mercy, as He promised our fathers, Abraham and his descendants, forever."

The time for Mary's baby to be born was drawing near. Around this time, news came that the Roman emperor, Caesar Augustus, had sent an order to all people in the countries that were under Roman rule. The order stated that everyone's name must be put on a list, in order to pay taxes. But first, each person had to go to his birthplace to register, to have his name written on this list called a census.

Joseph and Mary also needed to be listed on the census. Joseph was of the family of King David, whose birthplace was Bethlehem. Therefore Joseph and Mary prepared for their passage down to Bethlehem, a journey almost as long as Mary's trip had been when she visited her cousin Elizabeth.

Joseph was concerned. Mary was so close to giving birth, and their journey would be difficult. He prayed for strength. From Nazareth, Joseph and Mary traveled down the mountains to the river Jordan. They followed the long river almost to its end. At that point, they climbed up the mountains of Judah. Then, at last, they reached the little town of Bethlehem.

"Finally," Joseph said, "we are here. Soon we will be safe and sound in one of the inns." Mary gave him a sleepy smile. "Joseph," she said, "thank you for leading us here. I am so grateful."

The stars shone dimly that night in Bethlehem as Joseph and Mary, weary from travel, searched for a place to rest. The town bustled with visitors who had come to have their names written on the emperor's list. No one knew that Mary was about to become the mother of the Son of God. Everywhere Joseph and Mary went, people said, "There is no room for you."

Mary paused to feel the cool wind on her face and the ache in her weary bones. She knew that her time had come. She would give birth that very night.

Joseph tried again to find a place for Mary to rest. He approached a small inn and knocked at the door. When a man answered the door, Joseph asked, "Do you have a room where we can sleep tonight? My wife is with child; she will have the baby at any moment."

"I'm truly sorry," the innkeeper said. "My inn is full. There is no room for you here." Joseph blinked back his tears. "O God," he thought, "what am I going to do? How can I help Mary?"

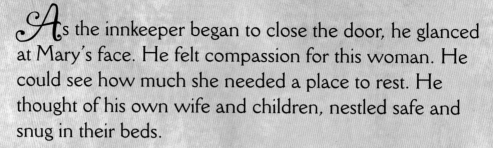

As the innkeeper began to close the door, he glanced at Mary's face. He felt compassion for this woman. He could see how much she needed a place to rest. He thought of his own wife and children, nestled safe and snug in their beds.

The innkeeper swung the door back open and turned to Joseph. "I have a stable outside in back of the inn. If you like, you can sleep there with the animals," he said. "I'm sorry, but it's the best I can do for you."

Joseph looked at Mary, who nodded at him with a grateful smile. "Thank you," Joseph said. "Thank you for your kindness." Joseph and Mary went to the stable where Mary could rest, surrounded by the comforting sounds of the farm animals. Joseph made a bed for Mary out of the softest hay he could find.

There, in the stable in Bethlehem, Mary gave birth to her baby son, Jesus, and she was filled with joy. She wrapped him in swaddling clothes to keep him warm. Somewhere in the back of the stable Joseph found a manger that was used to feed the cows and the oxen. He emptied it, carefully cleaned it, and used it to make a tiny bed for the baby. Mary laid her newborn son in the manger and watched over him as he slept.

That night, under the same starry sky, there were shepherds keeping watch over their flocks of sheep in the nearby fields. Some guarded the sheep, tending to their comfort, while others gathered to share stories, and to rest. Suddenly the night sky exploded with light, shining around the shepherds, and they were struck with fear. Out of the glorious light, an angel of the Lord appeared to them and declared,

"Do not be afraid, for behold, I proclaim to you good news of great joy for all people! For today in Bethlehem, the city of David, a savior is born for you who is Christ the Lord. You will find him wrapped in swaddling clothes, lying in a manger."

Suddenly a great gathering of heavenly angels joined the first angel. Together they proclaimed their praises of God, singing, "Glory to God in the highest, and on earth, peace to those on whom His favor rests."

As the angels returned to heaven, the shepherds looked at each other in shock and awe. Was it true that the Messiah, the savior, had come at last? Could he possibly have arrived so near to their own humble homes? "Hurry!" the shepherds said to one another. "Let us go now to Bethlehem. We must see this child!"

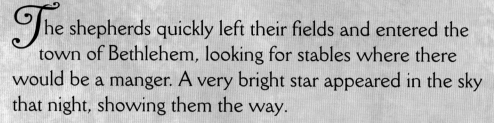

The shepherds quickly left their fields and entered the town of Bethlehem, looking for stables where there would be a manger. A very bright star appeared in the sky that night, showing them the way.

"Look!" cried a young shepherd boy. "Over here, in back of the inn!" The shepherds followed the boy to a rough stable, which was bathed in the starlight. There they found Joseph and Mary watching over the baby asleep in the manger. The shepherds looked at the child, and were filled with awe and wonder once again. They knelt down and honored the newborn babe.

"A most amazing thing happened to us!" the shepherds exclaimed to a puzzled Mary and Joseph. "We were in the field, and an angel came and told us that the Messiah was born this night!"

The next day, the shepherds told the villagers all about what had happened, and repeated the angel's words. Their story amazed everyone who heard it. The news spread like wildfire, and a great excitement filled the air. Many people in Bethlehem had seen the star that night, and wondered what it meant. Mary smiled at all these things and kept them quietly in her heart.

Having seen the child, the shepherds returned to their field, praising God for all they had seen and heard.

The Law of God commanded that every Jewish family must present their first male child at the age of 40 days to the Lord in the Temple. Joseph and Mary, too, brought their infant Jesus to the Temple in Jerusalem.

Now there lived in Jerusalem at that time a very old holy man named Simeon. The Holy Spirit had promised Simeon that he would not die until he had seen the Messiah of the Lord, whose coming had been foretold in the Scriptures.

That day the Spirit of the Lord urged Simeon to go to the Temple. He went, and when Joseph and Mary came in to the Temple with the baby Jesus, Simeon saw the child and felt a thrill of excitement run through his body. The Lord let him know that this was the Christ who had been promised. Simeon took Jesus in his arms and blessed God, saying:

"Now, Master, you may let your servant go in peace, according to your word. For my eyes have seen your salvation, which you have prepared in the sight of all the peoples; a light to lighten the Gentiles, and glory for your people Israel."

Mary and Joseph were amazed at what was being said about Jesus. Simeon blessed them, and said to Mary, "Behold, this child is destined for the fall and rise of many in Israel. A sword shall pierce your heart also, so that the thoughts of many hearts may be revealed."

A few days after Jesus was born, wise men, called Magi, also came to visit him. They had traveled a long way on camels and horses to Jerusalem.

When they arrived in the Holy City, the Magi asked, "Where is he who has been born King of the Jews? For we have seen his star in the East and have come to worship him." When King Herod, the old ruler of Judea under Caesar, heard this, he was afraid. Herod asked the chief priests to tell him where the Messiah was to be born. "In Bethlehem," they told him, "for thus it is written in God's Word:

'And you, Bethlehem, land of Judah, are by no means least among the rulers of Judah; since from you shall come a ruler, who is to shepherd my people Israel.'"

King Herod called the Magi and asked them when they had first seen the star. Then he sent them to Bethlehem. "Go," Herod said, "and search diligently for the child." He added, "When you find him, let me know, so I can go and worship him too."

However, Herod did not intend to worship the Messiah. He did not want anyone but himself to rule the people. Secretly, old King Herod had an evil plan to kill the baby. But first he had to find out where the infant king was.

After meeting with King Herod, the Magi set out on their journey. They were overjoyed that night to see the star going before them. They earnestly followed it again, this time all the way to Bethlehem. There the star stopped and shone over the place where Jesus was.

The Magi entered and saw the baby with his mother, Mary, and Joseph, her husband, resting together with the animals in the stable. The Magi knew at once that this child was a king. They rejoiced, they praised God, and they bowed low to worship the baby as the Lord, the Messiah. Then the Magi opened their treasures and offered to Jesus gifts of gold, frankincense, and myrrh. These were gifts worthy of a king, as was their custom.

After a joy-filled day, that night God warned the Magi in a dream not to go back to King Herod. They were not to tell Herod where the baby Jesus lived. So the Magi mounted their camels and left for their country by a different way. For a little while, the infant king was safe.

After the Magi had departed for home, God sent a warning to Joseph. The angel of the Lord appeared to him in a dream. "Rise," the angel commanded Joseph. "Your family is in danger. Take the child and his mother and flee to Egypt, and stay there until I tell you to come back. Herod is going to search for the child to destroy him."

Joseph awoke with a start. Because of his strong faith, he believed that the angel came from God, and he trusted what the angel said. So late that night, Joseph took his wife and Jesus and the donkey, and they set out on the long journey to Egypt.

Mary bravely followed Joseph's decisions. She knew that God would guide him, and show them the way. God was faithful, and throughout all the history of Israel, He always delivered His people from their enemies. So together the little family crossed over into Egypt, and found a place to stay, where they would be safe.

After some time, the angel of the Lord once again appeared to Joseph in a dream. The angel said, "Rise, take the child and his mother and return to the land of Israel. King Herod has died, and there is no more danger."

When Joseph learned that Herod's son was ruling over Bethlehem, he decided not to return there. Instead, Joseph and Mary packed their few belongings and headed back with Jesus to their little home in Nazareth.

The trip back home from Egypt was a long one for the little family. When Joseph, Mary and Jesus finally reached Nazareth, their family and friends welcomed them with open arms. They were so happy to be together again! When Joseph and Mary had left Nazareth, they were a newly married young couple, and Jesus was not yet even born. When Joseph and Mary returned, they had a delightful young boy.

In Nazareth, Joseph, Mary, and Jesus were a happy family. The child grew and became strong, filled with wisdom, and the favor of God was upon him. Joseph taught Jesus about his trade of carpentry, and Jesus learned quickly. The family worked together, laughed together, sang together, and prayed together. The Holy Spirit was with them.

Mary looked fondly at her son and said tenderly, "Jesus, you have filled us with joy, and you have shown us all how much God loves us."

Jesus smiled back at Mary. "Mother," he said, "I love you too!"

"*In* those days a decree went out from Caesar Augustus that the whole world should be enrolled. … So all went to be enrolled, each to his own town. And Joseph too went up from Galilee from the town of Nazareth to Judea, to the city of David that is called Bethlehem, because he was of the house and family of David, to be enrolled with Mary, his betrothed, who was with child. While they were there, the time came for her to have her child, and she gave birth to her firstborn son. She wrapped him in swaddling clothes and laid him in a manger, because there was no room for them in the inn.

"Now there were shepherds in that region living in the fields and keeping the night watch over their flock. The angel of the Lord appeared to them and the glory of the Lord shone around them, and they were struck with great fear. The angel said to them, 'Do not be afraid; for behold, I proclaim to you good news of great joy that will be for all the people. For today in the city of David a savior has been born for you who is Messiah and Lord. And this will be a sign for you: you will find an infant wrapped in swaddling clothes and lying in a manger.'

"And suddenly there was a multitude of the heavenly host with the angel, praising God and saying: 'Glory to God in the highest and on earth peace to those on whom his favor rests.' When the angels went away from them to heaven, the shepherds said to one another, 'Let us go, then, to Bethlehem to see this thing that has taken place, which the Lord has made known to us.' So they went in haste and found Mary and Joseph, and the infant lying in the manger." –LUKE 2:1, 3-12